D1037246

TYPHOID FEVER
Dirty Food, Dirty Water!

by William Caper

Consultant: Andi L. Shane, M.D., M.P.H., M.Sc.

BEARPORT
PUBLISHING

New York, New York

Credits

Cover and Title Page, © Jay Directo/AFP/Getty Images; 4–5, © Oyster Bay Historical Society, Postcard Collection, 00.0.695(Detail); 5, © Columbia University Archives (RBML) Butler Library, New York, NY; 6L, © The National Library of Medicine, Bethesda, Maryland; 6R, Courtesy of The New York Public Library; 7, © American Heritage Publishing Company; 8L, © American Heritage Publishing Company; 8R, © The National Library of Medicine, Bethesda, Maryland; 9, © New York City Municipal Archives, Department of Public Charities Collection, Image no. 2000; 10, © The Minnesota Historical Society; 11L, © Dennis Kunkel Microscopy, Inc./Visuals Unlimited, Inc.; 11R, © jcjgphotography/Shutterstock; 12, © Mike Devlin/Photo Researchers, Inc.; 13, © Paula Bronstein/Getty Images; 14, © Jim Varney/Photo Researchers, Inc.; 15, © The National Library of Medicine, Bethesda, Maryland; 16L, © Bubbles Photolibrary/Alamy; 16R, © Colin Cuthbert/Photo Researchers, Inc.; 17, © Virginia Commonwealth University, Tompkins-McCaw Library Special Collections and Archives; 18, © Stock Connection/SuperStock; 19L, © Jim Varney/Photo Researchers, Inc.; 19R, © Mark Penny/iStockphoto; 21, © Dennis M. Sabangan/epa/Corbis; 22T, © Courtesy of The New York Public Library; 22B, © Bettmann/Corbis; 23T, Courtesy of Bubbles Yadow; 23B, © Christopher Payne Photography; 24, © Susan Kane; 25, © Peter Macdiarmid/Getty Images; 26, © Jonas Sulit/Xinhua/Zuma Press/Newscom; 27L, © Wayne Hutchinson/Alamy; 27R, © Compassion Care Foundation-Kalaiti Village Water Well Project; 28L, © Peter V. S. Bond; 28R, © University of Washington Libraries, Special Collections Division; 29, Courtesy of Wikipedia.

Publisher: Kenn Goin
Editorial Director: Adam Siegel
Creative Director: Spencer Brinker
Design: Dawn Beard Creative
Photo Researcher: Jennifer Bright

Library of Congress Cataloging-in-Publication Data

Caper, William.
  Typhoid fever : dirty food, dirty water! / by William Caper ; consultant, Andi Shane.
    p. cm. — (Nightmare plagues)
  Includes bibliographical references and index.
  ISBN-13: 978-1-936088-04-1 (library binding)
  ISBN-10: 1-936088-04-5 (library binding)
  1. Typhoid fever—Juvenile literature. I. Title.
  RA644.T8C37 2011
  614.5'112—dc22
                                        2010005828

Copyright © 2011 Bearport Publishing Company, Inc. All rights reserved. No part of this publication may be reproduced in whole or in part, stored in a retrieval system, or transmitted in any form or by any means, electronic, mechanical, photocopying, recording, or otherwise, without written permission from the publisher.

For more information, write to Bearport Publishing Company, Inc., 101 Fifth Avenue, Suite 6R, New York, New York 10003. Printed in the United States of America in North Mankato, Minnesota.

062010
042110CGB

10 9 8 7 6 5 4 3 2 1

Contents

Typhoid Fever Strikes

In the summer of 1906, banker Charles Warren and his family rented a house in Oyster Bay, Long Island. They wanted to have a relaxing vacation by the beach. Little did they know, however, that on August 27, disease would strike their summer home. On that day, Warren's daughter, Margaret, came down with a **fever**. Within a week, five more people got sick. It soon became clear that **typhoid fever** was taking over the household.

This is the house in Oyster Bay where the Warren family spent the summer in 1906.

Typhoid fever was a common, and often deadly, disease in the United States in the early 1900s. In New York City alone, almost 3,500 people became ill with typhoid in 1906, and 639 of them died.

Luckily, nobody died from the disease. However, the owners of the home wanted to find out how the **outbreak** had started. So they hired typhoid expert George Soper. He checked the food, water, and milk in the house for typhoid **germs**. He didn't find any.

Then Soper learned that the Warrens had hired a new cook about three weeks before the illness struck. Could she be the cause? The cook, named Mary Mallon, had quit before Soper arrived. The family said she was perfectly healthy. Still, Soper wanted to learn more about her.

George Soper had investigated the sources of other typhoid outbreaks before he was hired to study the one in Oyster Bay.

Searching for Mary

Soper looked into Mary Mallon's past. He discovered that since 1900, she had worked as a cook for seven families. Twenty-two people in those households had caught typhoid after Mary had prepared food for them. One girl had died.

Soper knew he had to track Mary down. In March 1907, he found her working as a cook for a family in New York City. Soper asked Mary for samples of her **stool**, blood, and **urine**. He told her they would be tested for typhoid germs.

TYPHOID FEVER.

This Notice is Posted in Compliance with Law

"Every person who shall wilfully tear down, remove or deface any notice posted in compliance with law, shall be fined not more than seven dollars."---GENERAL STATUTES OF CONNECTICUT, REVISION OF 1902, SECTION 1173.

Town Health Officer.

Town Health Officer.

Town Health Officer.

In the early 1900s, health officials posted signs like this one on buildings to warn people about the presence of typhoid fever.

Mary Mallon was born in Ireland, in 1869, and came to the United States as a teenager.

Most typhoid sufferers have **symptoms**— they look and feel very sick. However, some people who have typhoid germs in their bodies never show symptoms and are healthy. These people are called **carriers**. Mary Mallon was a carrier.

Mary didn't believe she was spreading the disease. After all, she had never been sick with typhoid. She was also **offended** by Soper's request. Mary picked up a large carving fork and threatened to stab Soper if he didn't leave. Terrified, he dashed out of the house. Soper realized he needed help.

This illustration shows Mary threatening George Soper after he told her that she might have typhoid.

A Mystery Is Solved

Soper decided to contact the New York City Health Department. They sent Dr. Sara Josephine Baker and five police officers to the home where Mary was working. Mary saw them coming, though. By the time they entered the house, she had disappeared.

The police looked everywhere for Mary. Finally, after searching for five hours, they found her—hidden in a closet. She would not leave the house peacefully, though. Mary screamed and shouted as policemen forced her into an ambulance.

This illustration shows police officers arresting Mary Mallon.

On the ambulance ride to the hospital, Dr. Sara Josephine Baker (right) had to sit on Mary to keep her still. "It was like being in a cage with an angry lion," she said.

At a nearby hospital, doctors tested Mary's stool and found typhoid germs. Health officials wanted to stop Mary from spreading typhoid, so they **quarantined** her. She was placed in a cottage near a hospital on New York City's North Brother Island. Mary was forced to stay there for almost three years.

Mary lived in this cottage on North Brother Island, in New York City's East River.

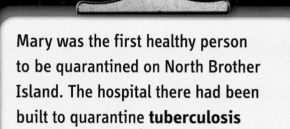

Mary was the first healthy person to be quarantined on North Brother Island. The hospital there had been built to quarantine **tuberculosis** patients. Like typhoid, tuberculosis can easily spread from person to person.

This map shows the island where Mary was quarantined after she was arrested.

How Does Typhoid Spread?

At the time that Mary was quarantined, typhoid fever was a big problem in the United States. About 200,000 Americans became ill from it every year. Around 35,000 of them died. How did the deadly disease spread to so many people?

Typhoid is caused by tiny germs called **bacteria**. People with typhoid release the bacteria in their waste. In places with poor **sanitation**, the bacteria in human waste can get into rivers and lakes. People who get their drinking water from these **infected** places may become sick.

This photograph from the late 1800s shows the Mississippi River filled with human waste and other pollution.

If people who have typhoid don't clean their hands after using the bathroom, they can also pass on the disease. How? The bacteria from their waste may be on their hands, which can infect things they touch, such as food. If healthy people eat this food, then they can get sick, too.

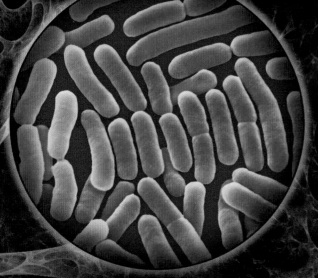

Salmonella typhi (S. typhi), shown here in close-up, is the name of the bacteria that cause typhoid fever.

Hand washing can help prevent the spread of typhoid fever and many other diseases.

Mary Mallon often served the Warren family a dessert of ice cream and sliced peaches. This was one way Mary could have spread typhoid. Cooking food at a high enough temperature and for a long enough time will kill typhoid bacteria. The dessert Mary prepared, however, was not cooked.

A Terrible Disease

In the early 1900s, many Americans were afraid of catching typhoid. Its terrible symptoms creep up slowly on victims over several weeks. During the first week of illness, patients have a rising fever. They may also have pounding headaches and stomach pain with **constipation**.

In the second week, the fever peaks at around 104°F (40°C). This is much higher than a person's normal body temperature of 98.6°F (37°C). People may get a **rash**, too.

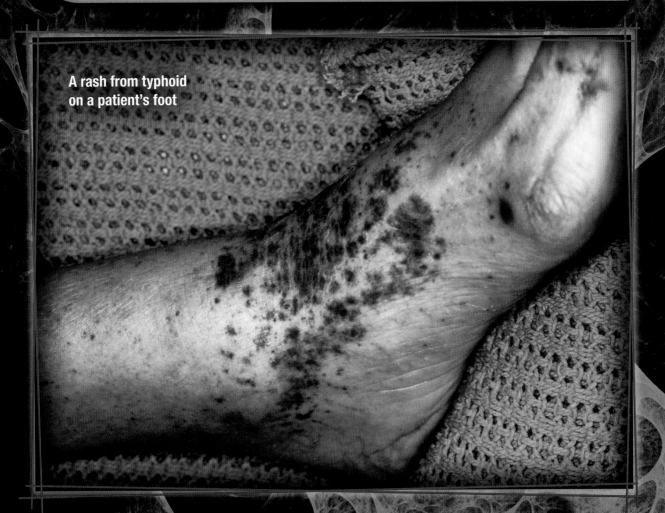

A rash from typhoid on a patient's foot

Patients with typhoid may become weak and **delirious**. As a result, they may not know where they are, or even who they are. They might see or hear things that aren't real.

During the third week, diarrhea may develop, especially in children. People with typhoid usually feel better by the fourth week. Some patients, however, may feel sick for several months.

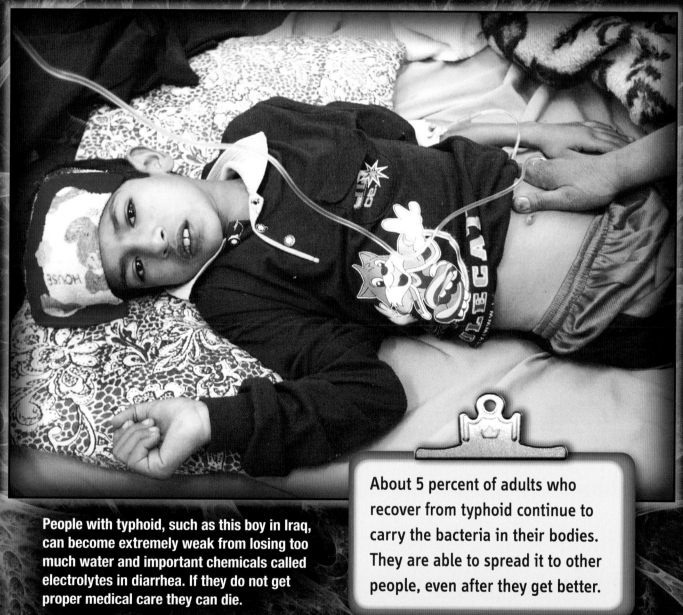

People with typhoid, such as this boy in Iraq, can become extremely weak from losing too much water and important chemicals called electrolytes in diarrhea. If they do not get proper medical care they can die.

About 5 percent of adults who recover from typhoid continue to carry the bacteria in their bodies. They are able to spread it to other people, even after they get better.

Vaccines Help Fight Typhoid

In 1896, European scientists had a breakthrough in the fight against the deadly disease when they created a typhoid **vaccine**. A vaccine is a liquid that contains the dead or weakened germs that cause a disease. It offers some protection from an illness. How does a vaccine work?

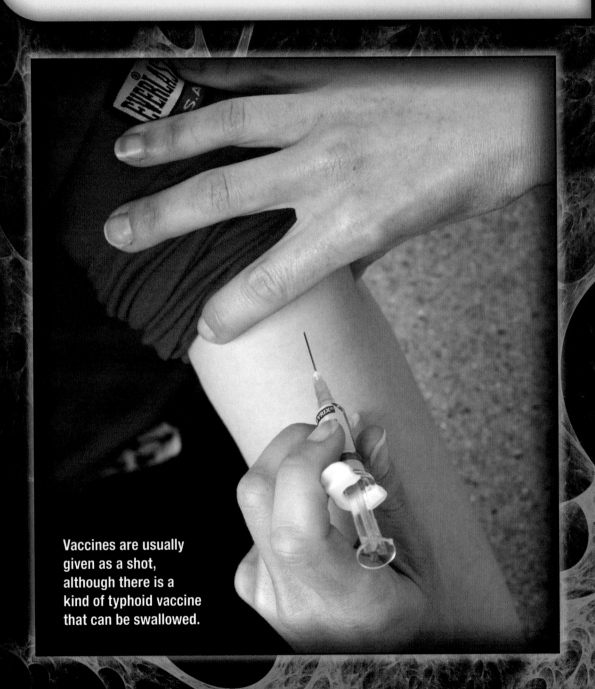

Vaccines are usually given as a shot, although there is a kind of typhoid vaccine that can be swallowed.

After a typhoid vaccine is given to a person, it "tricks" the body into thinking it has been infected with typhoid fever. As a result, the body makes a kind of protein called an **antibody** that helps fight the bacteria. If typhoid bacteria later enter the body, the antibodies recognize them and destroy them so that the person does not get sick.

This photo shows U.S. Army soldiers during World War I (1914–1918) being vaccinated against typhoid fever.

In 1911, Dr. Frederick F. Russell started a program in which he gave typhoid vaccine shots to the entire U.S. Army. One scientist estimated that without the vaccine, there would have been 500,000 typhoid **infections** among U.S. soldiers during World War I. Instead, there were only about 1,500.

Treating the Sick

Today, doctors have even more weapons to fight typhoid. If a person catches the illness, the most common way to treat it is with medicines called **antibiotics**. They kill or slow the growth of the typhoid bacteria in the body.

Typhoid antibiotic

If doctors think a sick person might have typhoid, they'll test the person's blood or stool to see if *S. typhi* bacteria are present. If so, they'll give the patient an antibiotic.

People who have typhoid can be given antibiotics even though they don't feel sick. The medicines help prevent them from spreading the disease to others.

People taking antibiotics for typhoid usually start to feel better in a couple of days. Even while they are taking the medicine, however, typhoid patients still have to do certain things to prevent spreading the disease. For example, they should always wash their hands with soap and warm water or a hand gel after using the bathroom. They also shouldn't prepare food for others.

This 1908 cartoon shows how much people feared typhoid before vaccines and antibiotics were in common use. Without these medicines to treat typhoid, up to 30 percent of its victims die.

Travelers Beware!

Typhoid spreads only in places where human waste comes into contact with food or drinking water. Some countries, such as the United States, Canada, Japan, England, and Australia, have **plumbing** systems that keep dirty water from toilets and sinks separate from water that is used for drinking, cooking, and washing. These countries also add chlorine to their water supplies. This chemical kills harmful bacteria, including typhoid. As a result, there is plenty of clean water.

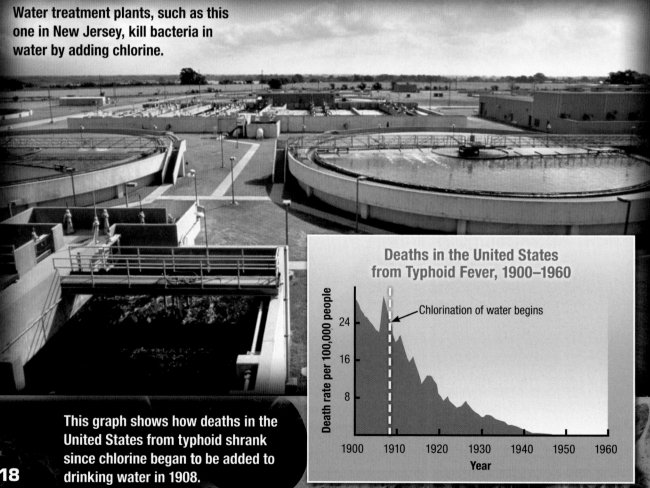

Water treatment plants, such as this one in New Jersey, kill bacteria in water by adding chlorine.

Deaths in the United States from Typhoid Fever, 1900–1960

Chlorination of water begins

Death rate per 100,000 people

24

16

8

1900 1910 1920 1930 1940 1950 1960

Year

This graph shows how deaths in the United States from typhoid shrank since chlorine began to be added to drinking water in 1908.

People who live in countries with clean water sources are generally safe from typhoid infections. However, they can catch the disease if they travel to places in the world where there is little clean water, including parts of India, Ethiopia, and Costa Rica. Doctors suggest that people traveling to these areas get vaccinated first.

When traveling to a country where typhoid infections are a problem, people should make sure that fruits and vegetables are washed using clean water.

Doctors remind people to get a vaccine before traveling to an area where typhoid is common.

Each year, about 400 people in the United States get typhoid fever. Most of these people have traveled to a foreign country within a month before getting sick.

Typhoid Around the World

Typhoid fever is still a danger for people who live in countries where it is hard to get clean water. Unfortunately, these countries also have little money for medicines to treat diseases. Every year, there are 16 to 33 million typhoid infections and about 200,000 deaths worldwide.

Typhoid Outbreaks

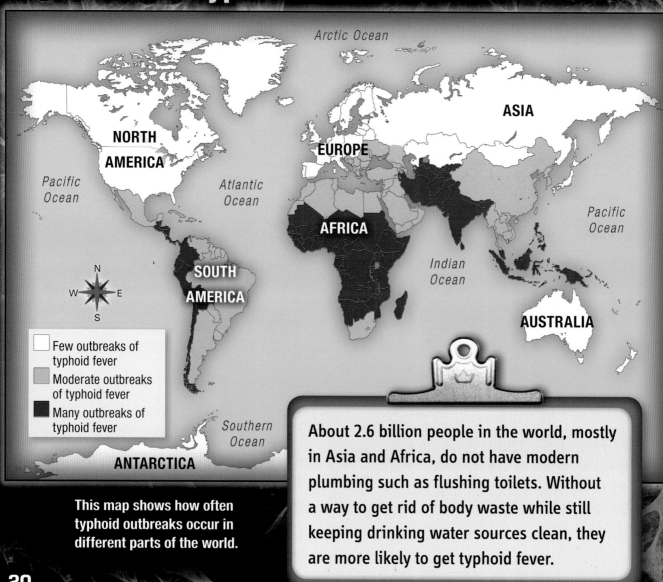

Arctic Ocean

ASIA

NORTH AMERICA

EUROPE

Pacific Ocean

Atlantic Ocean

Pacific Ocean

AFRICA

Indian Ocean

N
W E
S

SOUTH AMERICA

AUSTRALIA

Few outbreaks of typhoid fever

Moderate outbreaks of typhoid fever

Many outbreaks of typhoid fever

Southern Ocean

ANTARCTICA

This map shows how often typhoid outbreaks occur in different parts of the world.

About 2.6 billion people in the world, mostly in Asia and Africa, do not have modern plumbing such as flushing toilets. Without a way to get rid of body waste while still keeping drinking water sources clean, they are more likely to get typhoid fever.

A severe typhoid outbreak recently occurred in the Democratic Republic of Congo, in Africa. The outbreak lasted from September 2004 to January 2005. About 42,000 people got sick during this **plague**. More than 200 people died. To prevent more infections, local authorities encouraged people to wash their hands before handling food and after going to the bathroom.

In March 2008, there was an outbreak of typhoid in Calamba City, in the Philippines. More than 1,000 people were hospitalized. The cause was unclean water.

What Happened to Mary?

In Mary Mallon's time, even cooks did not usually wash their hands thoroughly before they prepared food. As a result, it was easy for Mary to spread typhoid germs. By 1910, she had been quarantined for about three years and was eager to be free. Even though she was still a carrier, health officials agreed to let her go if she didn't work as a cook.

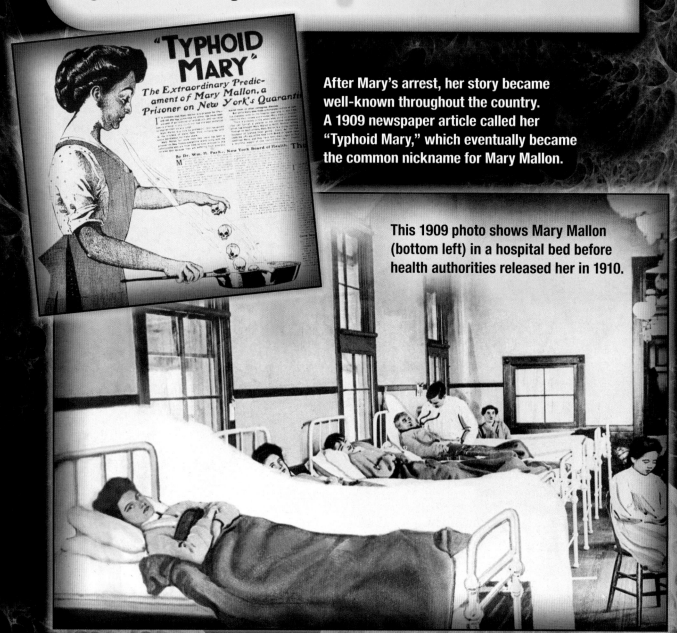

After Mary's arrest, her story became well-known throughout the country. A 1909 newspaper article called her "Typhoid Mary," which eventually became the common nickname for Mary Mallon.

This 1909 photo shows Mary Mallon (bottom left) in a hospital bed before health authorities released her in 1910.

For a while Mary made a living doing laundry, but that job paid less. So she changed her name to Mary Brown and went back to work as a cook. In 1915, while working at a hospital in New York City, she infected 25 people with typhoid. Two people died.

Authorities tracked the infection back to Mary. Again, she was arrested and quarantined on North Brother Island. She was forced to stay there for the rest of her life.

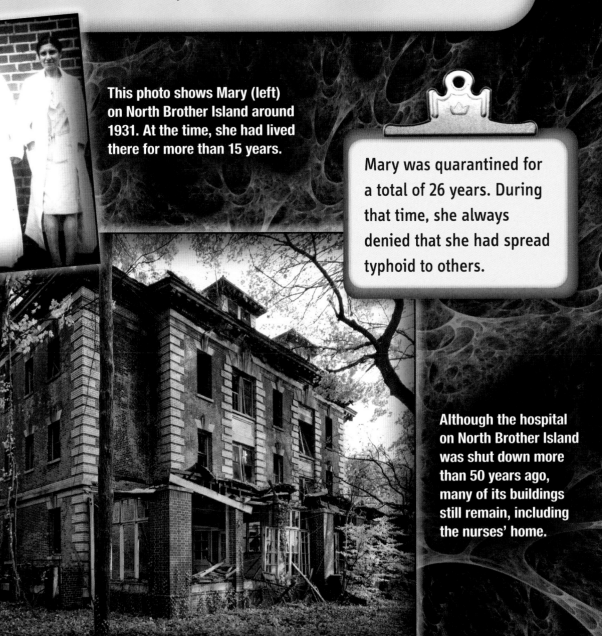

This photo shows Mary (left) on North Brother Island around 1931. At the time, she had lived there for more than 15 years.

Mary was quarantined for a total of 26 years. During that time, she always denied that she had spread typhoid to others.

Although the hospital on North Brother Island was shut down more than 50 years ago, many of its buildings still remain, including the nurses' home.

Mary Mallon Wasn't the Only One

Mary Mallon was the first known carrier of typhoid fever in the United States. She was also the most famous. Yet she wasn't the only healthy person spreading the disease in the United States during the early 1900s.

In 1938, at age 69, Mary Mallon died of pneumonia on North Brother Island. During her lifetime, she was known to have infected 47 people. Three of them died.

One of the most dangerous carriers was Tony Labella. In 1922, he was arrested for causing a typhoid outbreak in New Jersey while working on a farm. It resulted in 35 people getting sick. Three of the victims died. Earlier, Labella had caused an outbreak in which 87 people caught typhoid and two of them died.

In 1910, a guide in the Adirondack Mountains infected milk he handled before serving it to travelers. He spread typhoid to 38 people and caused two deaths. Reporters nicknamed him "Typhoid John."

The Battle Goes On

Even with better treatments for typhoid today, scientists still find the disease challenging. Sometimes typhoid germs change and the usual medicines may no longer be able to kill them. Typhoid bacteria that are harder to kill have been found in countries such as India, Pakistan, and Bangladesh.

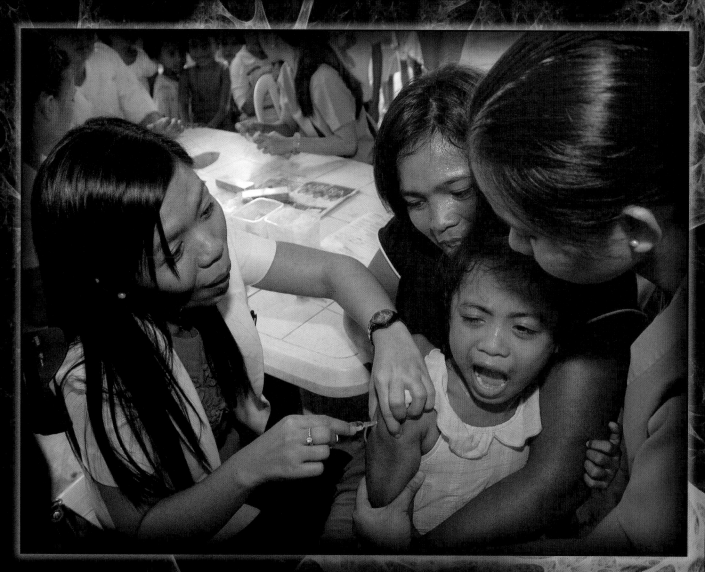

This girl in the Philippines may be unhappy now, but the typhoid vaccine she's receiving could save her life.

As the typhoid bacteria change, scientists work to develop new drugs to keep the illness under control. Health authorities also continue to educate people about the importance of keeping food clean and washing their hands after using the bathroom. In addition, many **charities** work to raise money to build wells that provide clean water in poor areas around the world.

Perhaps, with the help of these efforts, typhoid fever will one day be wiped out. Until then, the battle against this killer disease continues.

These people are trying out new wells built in Africa.

Today, the expression "Typhoid Mary" is used to describe someone who is a carrier of any disease that can easily spread from person to person.

Other Famous Typhoid Outbreaks

Until about 70 years ago, typhoid fever was common in places where it is now rare—such as the United States and England. When an outbreak occurred, health authorities worked hard to find the source as fast as they could.

Middletown, Connecticut, 1894

- Twenty-three students at Wesleyan University caught typhoid fever in 1894. Four of them died from the infection.

Wesleyan University's library

- The people who got sick had all eaten infected oysters from the nearby Quinnipiac River. At the time, human waste was dumped into the river, and the oysters probably became infected by it.

Maidstone, England, 1897–1898

- In September 1897, an outbreak of typhoid fever hit the town of Maidstone, in southeastern England. The outbreak lasted until January 1898.

- Nearly 2,000 people got sick. Of these, 143 died. It was the largest outbreak of typhoid fever ever reported in England.

- Infected drinking water was the cause of the outbreak.

Seattle, Washington, 1909

- In June 1909, a huge fair called the Alaska-Yukon-Pacific Exposition opened in Seattle, Washington. That September, the city was struck by an outbreak of typhoid fever.

- It was later determined that the outbreak was caused by infected drinking water being offered at the fair.

- In all, 511 people became infected with typhoid. Of those, 61 died. This was the last major outbreak of typhoid fever in Seattle.

Before the Alaska-Yukon-Pacific Exposition opened, the director of the fair said, "There is probably no city in the world that has a purer supply of water than Seattle."

Typhoid Fever Facts

Scientists identified the bacteria that cause typhoid fever in 1880. Here are some more facts about the disease.

Was It Typhoid?

Before scientists learned about typhoid bacteria, people didn't always know if an outbreak of a disease was typhoid fever. Historians and scientists have studied outbreaks of the past and believe many of them may have been typhoid infections.

- Around 430–426 B.C., a plague killed one third of the people in Athens, one of the most powerful cities in ancient Greece. Some scientists believe that this plague was an outbreak of typhoid fever.

- Typhoid fever has been present in America since at least the early 1600s. Some historians believe that in the English colony of Jamestown, Virginia, typhoid fever killed more than 6,000 settlers between 1607 and 1624.

Travelers' Warnings

People traveling to areas where typhoid fever is common are given the following advice by doctors:

- Eat only foods that are fully cooked and served hot. Eat and drink only dairy products that have been **pasteurized**. Pasteurizing and cooking kill bacteria on the foods.

- Eat only fruits and vegetables that you can wash with clean water and peel yourself.

- Do not eat food from street vendors.

- Drink beverages that have been bottled and sealed or that have been boiled for at least one minute, such as tea.

- Do not put ice in your drinks. The ice may contain typhoid bacteria.

Famous People Who Had Typhoid Fever

- Abigail Adams (1744–1818), wife of President John Adams—died

- Prince Albert (1819–1861), husband of Queen Victoria of England—died

- Louisa May Alcott (1832–1888), author of *Little Women*—survived

- Willie Lincoln (1850–1862) and Tad Lincoln (1853–1871), sons of President Abraham Lincoln—Willie died, Tad survived

- Wilbur Wright (1867–1912), inventor who, with his brother, Orville, built the first engine-powered airplane that could fly—died

Willie Lincoln was 11 years old when he died of typhoid fever on February 20, 1862.

Glossary

antibiotics (*an*-tee-bye-OT-iks) medicines that slow the growth of or kill bacteria

antibody (AN-ti-*bod*-ee) a protein made by the body that attaches itself to harmful germs to stop infections

bacteria (bak-TEER-ee-uh) tiny living things too small to be seen without a microscope; some bacteria are helpful, while others can cause disease

carriers (KA-ree-urz) healthy people who have the germs of a particular disease in their bodies and may spread it to others

charities (CHA-ruh-teez) groups that raise money or run programs for people in need of help

constipation (*kon*-sti-PAY-shuhn) having difficulty passing solid waste

delirious (di-LEER-ee-uhss) a state of mental confusion in which one may see or hear things that are not real

fever (FEE-vur) a rise in one's body temperature to a point that is above normal—98.6°F (37°C)

germs (JURMZ) tiny living things that can cause disease

infected (in-FEK-tid) filled with harmful germs

infections (in-FEK-shuhnz) illnesses caused by germs entering the body

offended (uh-FEN-did) to be upset by someone who does something that is not proper

outbreak (OUT-*brayk*) a sudden rise in the occurrence of something, such as a disease among a group of people

pasteurized (PASS-chuh-ryezd) to have been placed under a process that uses heat to kill germs

plague (PLAYG) a disease that spreads quickly and often kills many people

plumbing (PLUHM-ing) the pipes and other equipment that carry water into and out of a building

quarantined (KWOR-uhn-teend) separated from others in order to prevent the spread of a disease

rash (RASH) red spots that occur on the skin, often caused by an illness

sanitation (*san*-uh-TAY-shuhn) practices that promote cleanliness and the prevention of diseases in a community, including getting rid of body waste in a way that keeps drinking water clean

stool (STOOL) solid body waste

symptoms (SIMP-tuhmz) signs of a disease or other physical problem felt by a person; often feelings of pain or discomfort

tuberculosis (too-*bur*-kyuh-LOH-siss) a disease that usually affects the lungs and causes fever, coughing, and difficulty breathing

typhoid fever (TYE-foyd FEE-vur) a disease spread by bacteria that cause fever, diarrhea, weakness, and headaches

urine (YOOR-uhn) liquid waste produced by people and animals

vaccine (vak-SEEN) a medicine that protects a person from a particular disease

Bibliography

Bourdain, Anthony. *Typhoid Mary: An Urban Historical.* New York: Bloomsbury (2001).

Leavitt, Judith Walzer. *Typhoid Mary: Captive to the Public's Health.* Boston: Beacon Press (1996).

www.cdc.gov/ncidod/dbmd/diseaseinfo/TyphoidFever_g.htm (Centers for Disease Control and Prevention)

www.med.nyu.edu/patientcare/library/article.html?ChunkIID=11484 (NYU Langone Medical Center)

Read More

Altman, Linda Jacobs. *Plague and Pestilence: A History of Infectious Disease.* Berkeley Heights, NJ: Enslow (1998).

Barnard, Bryn. *Outbreak: Plagues That Changed History.* New York: Crown (2005).

Goldsmith, Connie. *Invisible Invaders: Dangerous Infectious Diseases.* Minneapolis, MN: Twenty-First Century Books (2006).

Ray, Kurt. *Typhoid Fever.* New York: Rosen (2001).

Learn More Online

To learn more about typhoid fever, visit
www.bearportpublishing.com/NightmarePlagues

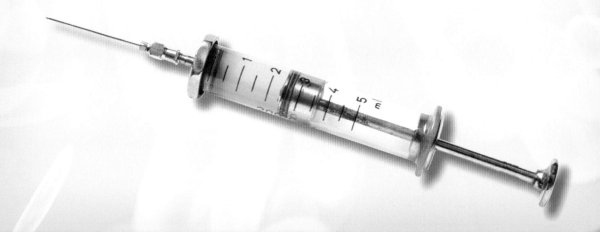

31

Index

About the Author

William Caper has written books about history, science, film, and many other topics. He lives in San Francisco, with his wife, Erin, and their dog, Face.